And So Can I!

Bill Gillham

Methuen Children's Books

This dog can paddle . . .

and so can I!

This pony can jump . . .

and so can I!

This pig can peep over a fence . . .

and so can I!

This cat can walk along a wall . . .

and so can I!

This lamb can drink from a bottle . . .

and so can I!

These puppies can feed from their mother . . .

and so can I!

This rabbit can wash her face . . .

and so can I!

These little ducks can swim . . .

and so can I!

This donkey can eat an apple . . .

and so can I!

This hamster can climb a ladder . . .

and so can I!

This horse can pull a cart . . .

and so can I!

This caterpillar can crawl . . .

and so can I!

This cat can lick . . .

and so can I!

This bird can hang on the bars . . .

and so can I!

But none of them . . .

can read a book like me!

Other early learning books by Bill Gillham

The First Words Picture Book
The Early Words Picture Book

Let's Look series
Let's Look for Numbers
Let's Look for Shapes
Let's Look for Opposites
Let's Look for Colours

Look and Talk series
What's the Difference?
Where Does It Go?
Can You See It?
What Can You Do?

What Happens Next?
All by Myself

Methuen Paired Reading Storybooks
Spencer's Spaghetti
Awful Arabella
Candy's Camel
Our Baby Bites
Nobody Likes My Spider
Dear Monster
Our Baby Throws Things
Bethy Wants a Blue Ice-Cream
Who Needs a Haircut?
Scribble Sam
Last One in Bed
Gertie's Goldfish

First published in Great Britain in 1987
by Methuen Children's Books Ltd
11 New Fetter Lane, London EC4P 4EE
Copyright © 1987 Bill Gillham

Printed in Hong Kong
by South China Printing Co.

ISBN 0 416 96090 1